Disciple Toolbox Kit

Disciple Toolbox Kit

by
Sharon Tuinder

with Illustrations by Anna Mauldin

Contents

Directions

To assemble the ToolBox

1) Remove the template from the front of the book and cut the pattern out.

2) Trace the pattern twice onto the poster board of your choice and cut them out. These will form the front and back of your toolbox.

3) Punch the holes around the outer edge of the front and back of your toolbox.

4) Using the string, yarn or ribbon of your choice, lace the two together. Tie a secure knot on both ends.

5) Write the words "Disciple Toolbox" on the front.

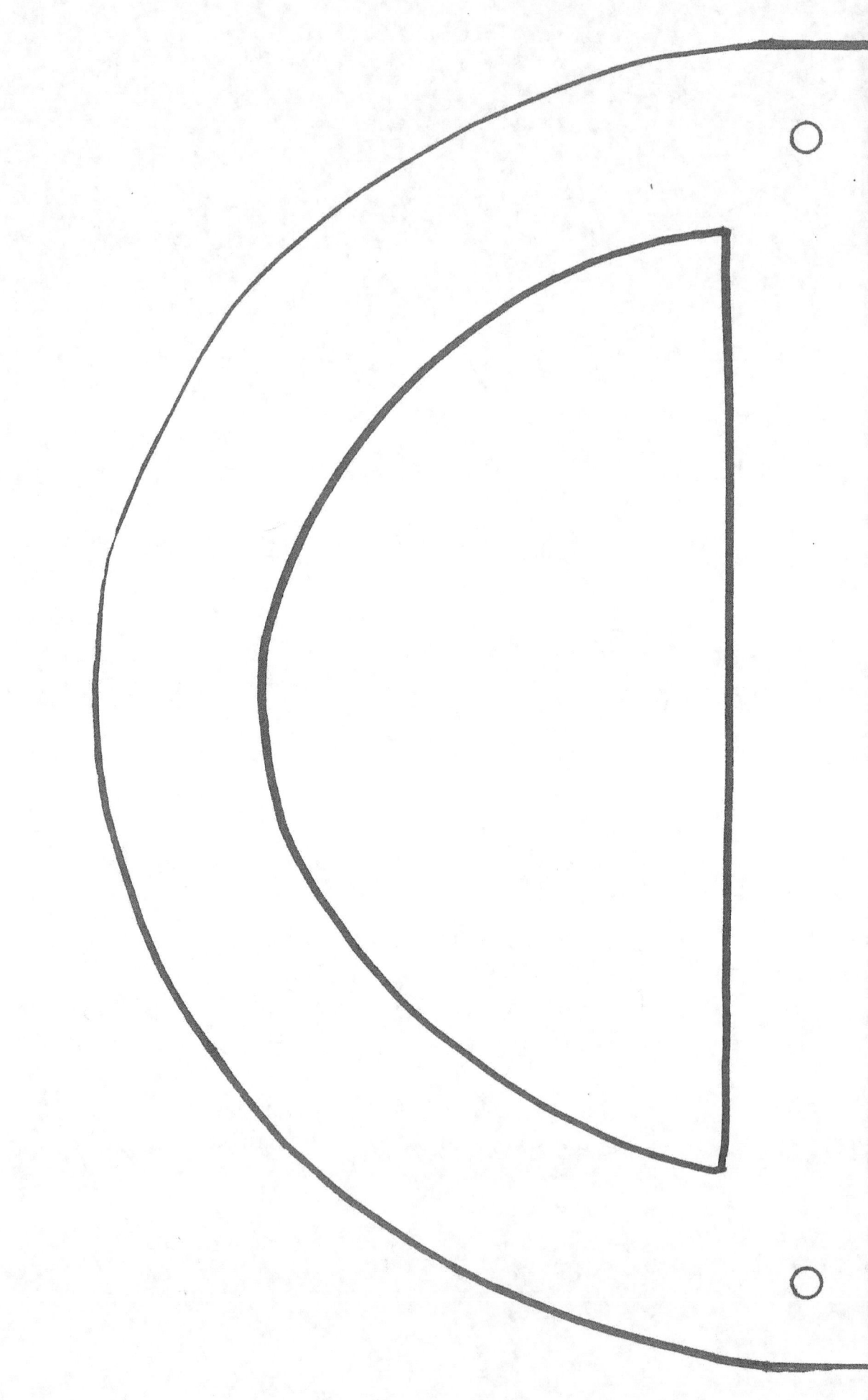

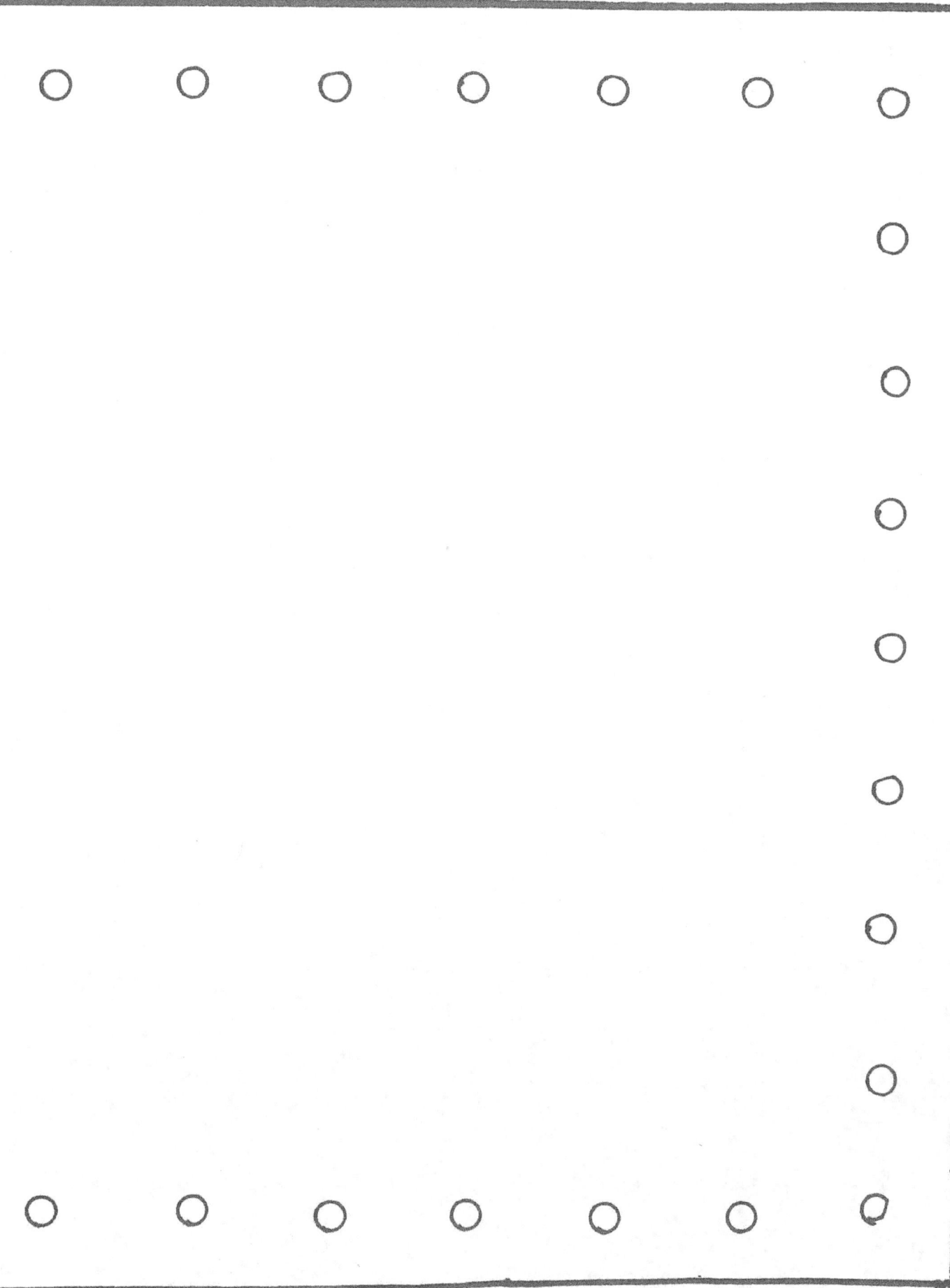

Key to the Secret Place

Prayer

Bible

Name of Jesus

Armor of God

Fruit of the Spirit

Gratitude

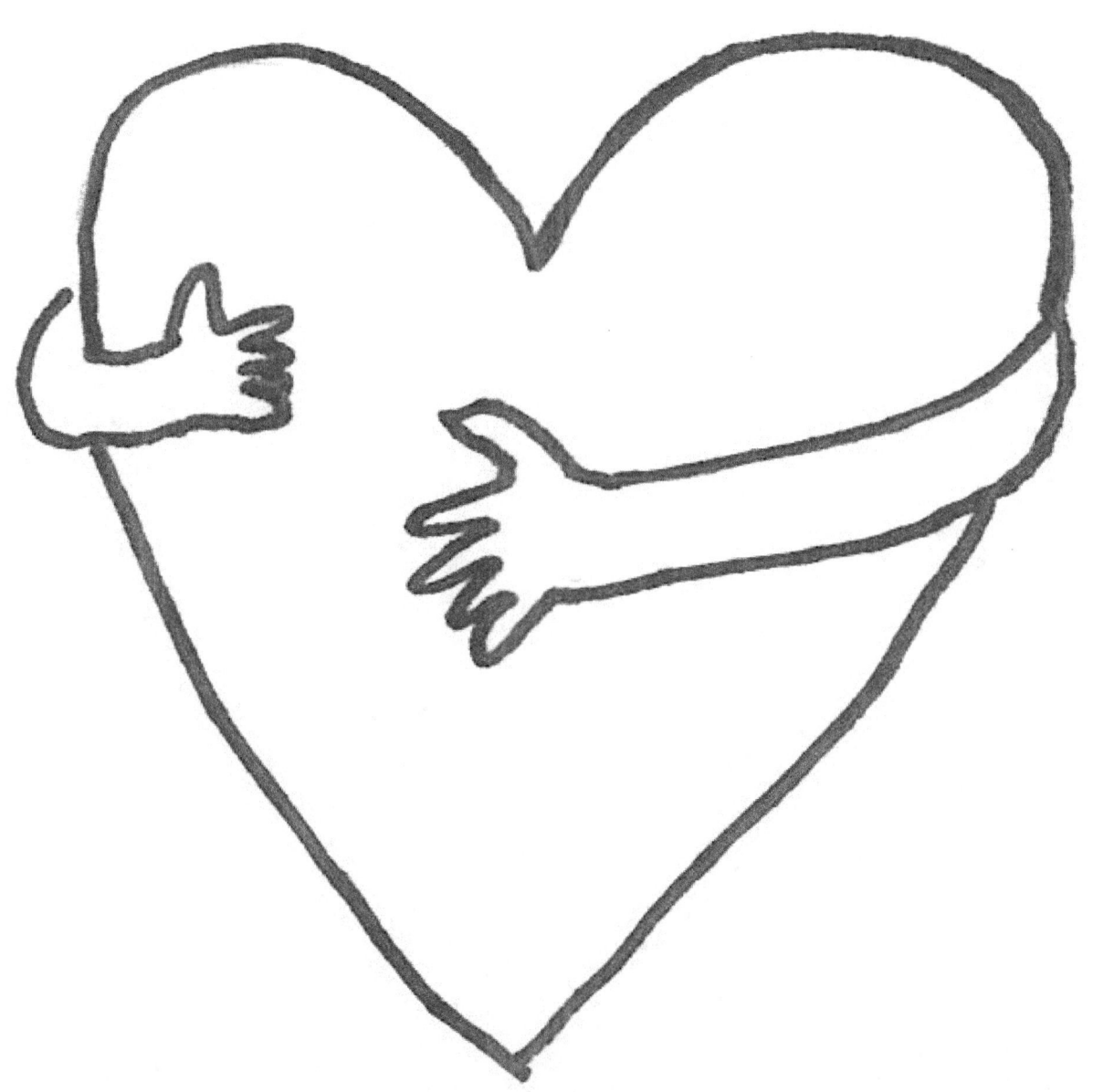

Giving

Forgiveness

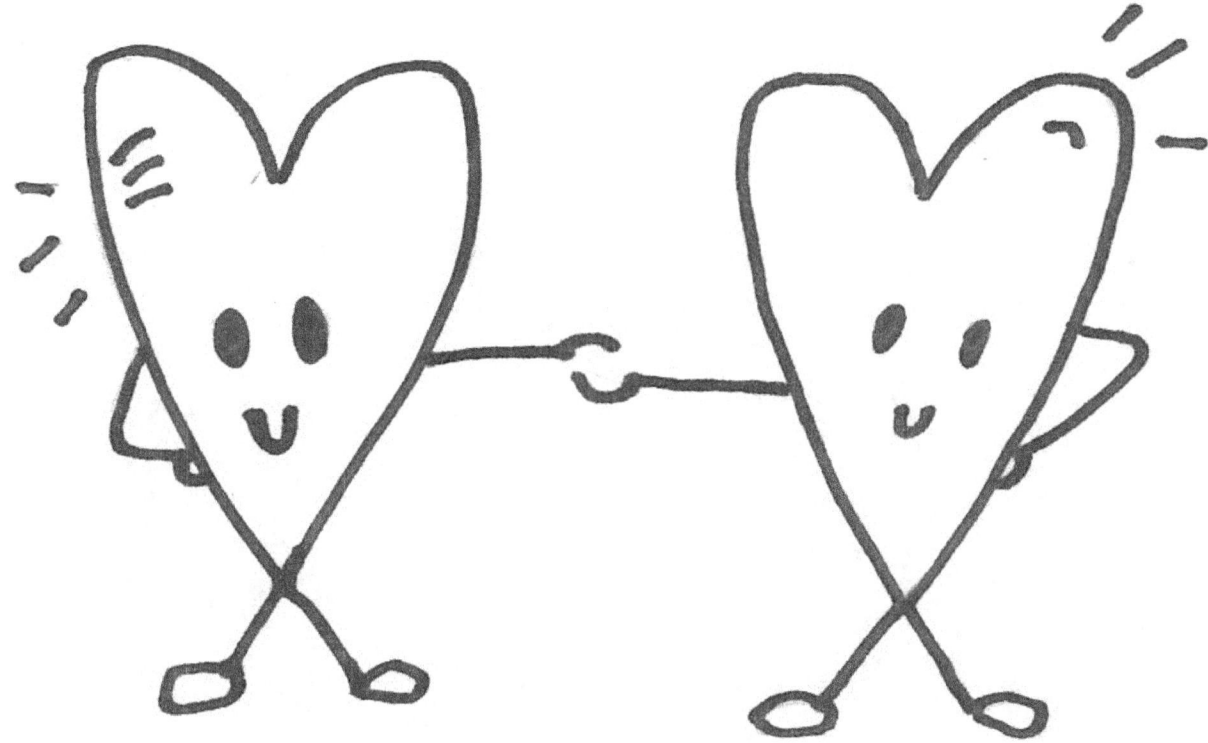

Get Ahead

Words That Lift Up

The 10 Commandments

Fear of the Lord

Fasting

Humility

Hands Up

Feet That Possess

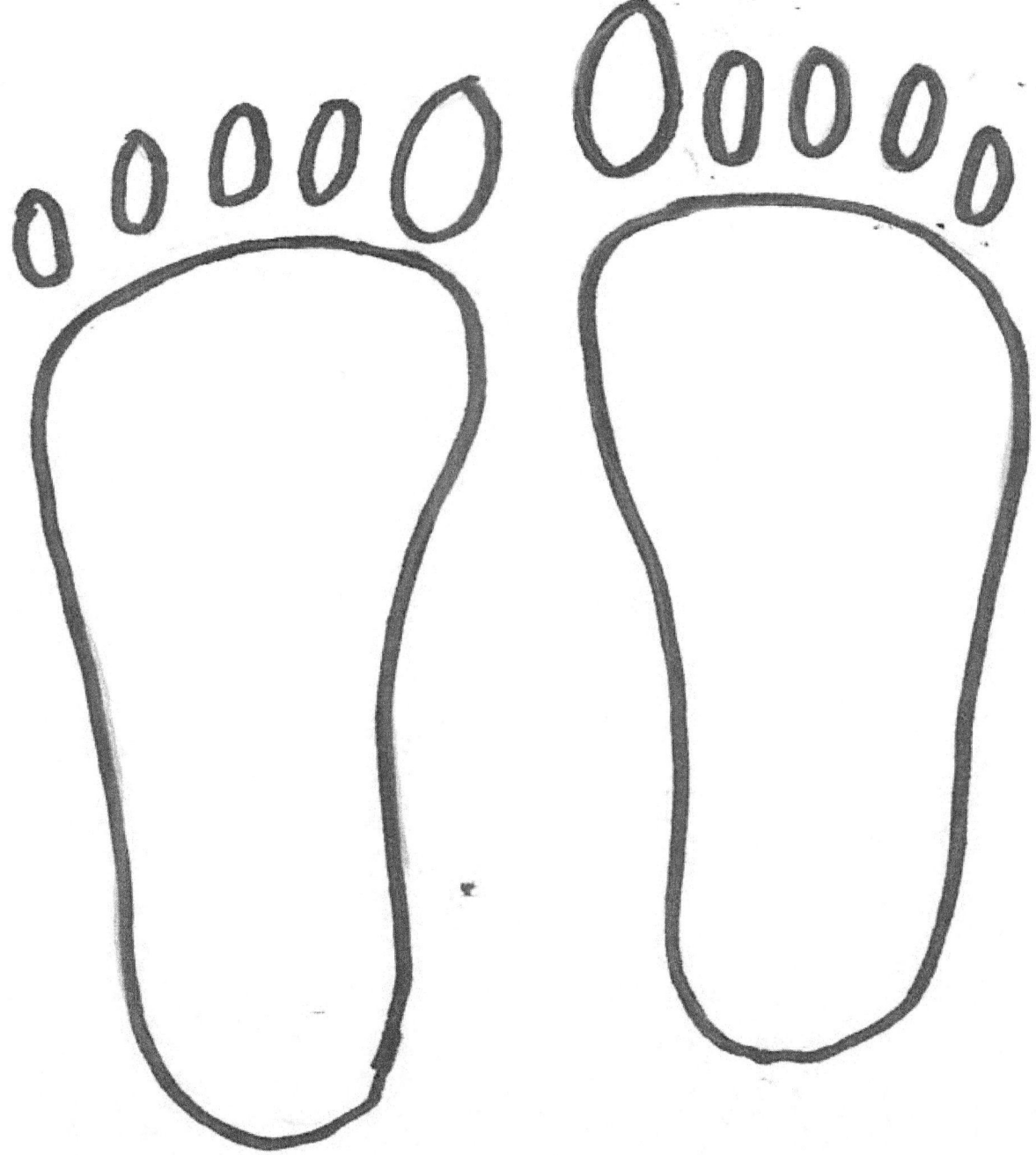

Heart That Breaks

Knees That Bow

Praise and Worship

Hunger And Thirst

Fellowship

Baptism

Pentecost Fire

Gifts of the Spirit

Your Cross

Witnessing

www.ingramcontent.com/pod-product-compliance
Lightning Source LLC
Chambersburg PA
CBHW081340120626
46546CB00011B/3431

9781961505087